HOW TO ACHIEVE A

HIGH

PERFORMING

MIND

HOW TO USE YOUR MIND TO FIND ANSWERS TO YOUR PROBLEMS

by

Kojo Kronzuwa Yankson

How To Achieve A High Performing Mind
Copyright 2016
Kojo Kronzuwa Yankson

Book Cover designed by: Samuel Budu-Manuel

Unless otherwise indicated, all scripture quotations are taken from the King James Version of the Holy Bible.

Published by
Centre for Leadership Influence
P.O. Box AT 636
Achimota - Ghana

For information or to order books, please email:
s_yankson@hotmail.com.
Tel: +1(301) 276-1956/+233(0)249477123

ISBN: 978-9988-2-3060-9
Printed in Ghana

FOREWORD

Every noble work seems impossible at first. It takes hard thinking and perseverance to succeed. It takes courage to work on something new and different – not to be part of the majority who are comfortable thinking and doing things in a familiar pattern. The invention of Ted Maiman in 1960 is a good example. In spite of all impediments, Ted Maiman successfully invented the first laser through careful thinking and staying with an idea he believed in. Today, lasers are used in diverse ways to improve productivity. You can cut through half an inch of steel with a laser: his is faster than any other means. Lasers are used for computer printers and extremely high-density information storage. The courage of young people – people like you who are not afraid to go ahead with ideas they believe in, despite discouragement – will similarly revolutionise the world after reading this book.

If you've never thought of being a great thinker and inventor like Ted Maiman, by the time you finish reading this book, you will begin setting scaffolds for your first invention. If you've never thought of being wealthy or

CEO of the company you work for, by the time you finish reading this book, you'll be planning your first corporate take-over. This book wells up positivity. It stirs the mind. It is a foot-to-the-floor pep talk of developing a can-do, go-for-it, don't-take-no-for-an-answer attitude to life.

You might say this is another of those self-help books. True, but unlike self-help books that tell you how to get ahead at the expense of others, this book will help you develop some skills required to form intelligent opinions, make good decisions, and determine the best course of action – as well as recognise when someone else's reasoning is faulty or manipulative. It will help you develop good reasoning abilities. And this does not happen in vacuum. It involves a lot of skills: Among them are the abilities to analyse, ask intelligent questions, think critically and control your thought. These indispensable skills to thinking and learning will equip you to make intelligent and informed decisions about issues in life.

Clear thinking requires an effort and doesn't always come naturally. But you will get better at it as you read this book.

This book stimulates your creative imagination through the concepts and techniques introduced in it.

Every chapter is vital. You will be fascinated by the astonishing knowledge and facts in this book. Irrespective of your background and how much instruction you have received on the subject, you are going to find surprising knowledge, as you proceed, chapter by chapter, through this book. In summary, this book will help you become an all-round learned person and help you develop your potential to the fullest.

Elijah Cooper Aggrey
M. Phil, Medical
Biochemistry

Contents

Acknowledgements

This book is the collective effort of many. Among them are Dr Deborah Alema-Mensah who is my constant support and Dr (Mrs) Ekua Anowah Amponsah Agyemang. I am grateful for their encouragement, vital criticisms and contributions.

Special thanks to Kwame Bein Yankson, Mr. John Kwabena Arthur, Dr. George Wiafe, Ing. Joseph X F Ribeiro, Nii Godson Quaya, Emanuel Mensah and Elijah Cooper Aggrey for taking time to edit and give suggestion that were vital for this publication

Finally, my appreciation to my mum: Elizabeth, siblings: Ato, Vida, Tony, Nana Kwaaba, Andrew, and friends: Charlse Wilson Andoh Pastor Crabbe and Maame Afua Acquah for their confidence in my abilities.

Chapter 1

The Mind

God rules the world but it is shaped by men. The men involved in shaping the world are men with great minds. The prospect of the world has and will always depend on the pace at which the human mind develops. The nineteenth century has seen some of the finest developed minds. These minds have facilitated the transformation of our world at a very rapid pace.

Thomas Edison invented the fluorescent tube. Joseph Aspdin invented the cement – Portland. Alexander Graham Bell and Elisha Gray are both credited with the invention of the telephone. These men are a few of the great minds that have helped to transform our world technologically.

These men were not born great. They attained greatness by exploring the power of their minds. It is said that Alexander Graham Bell was never satisfied with the success of his telephone invention. His laboratory notebooks revealed that he was driven by genuine and rare intellectual curiosity. This curiosity kept him regularly searching and wanting to discover and learn more.

The mind holds the central position in the life of every individual. It is the tool that coordinates the activities of all other tools of the human being. The worth of every man is determined and imprinted by his mind. Human beings lose their value and usefulness when their minds become faulty.

Everybody can aspire to become great, provided he or she can draw enough power from the mind. Helen Keller, born deaf and blind, is today a role model for millions. She overcame her challenges and became a source of inspiration to many through her books and inspirational lectures. Helen Keller's life and achievement depicts that every human being with a sane mind has a future, no matter the challenges.

The power of the mind is limitless. Despite all the great achievements by man, none has been able to maximise the full potential of the mind; not even Alexander the Great, Isaac Newton or Thomas Edison. Man keeps on improving on the exploits of his mind. Hence, the power of the mind can be described as infinite. The solution to whatever problem you are facing and will ever face is within the power of your mind to solve. The magnitude of your problem determines the amount of power that you need to draw from your mind.

The amount of power needed from the mind to build a canoe will be different from the power needed to build a ship. The magnitude of your desired result should equal the effort you put in accessing the power needed from the mind to fulfil it. Let us not be weary in exploring the mind for answers because it is the tool for acquiring answers.

God has equipped man with all he needs to undertake any venture on earth. Adam, without guidance, named all the animals in the Garden of Eden. Adam became the first fashion designer when fig leaves were in vogue in

Eden. If the mind is explored enough, all the answers to life's challenges can be found.

Jesus Christ rose to prominence at age 33. Tiger Woods made history as a golfer at the age of 20. Josiah became king of Israel at the age of eight and ruled for 31 years. Steven Paul Jobs the founder of Apple Incorporated became a millionaire before the age of 27. Singapore, 42 years old as at 2011, is the youngest country to gain the status of a first world country. There is no right age or time frame for people to come into prominence. The only time we enter prominence is when we exercise the power of our mind to such a point.

The mind is a tool; the fundamental tool among all tools. How well you operate any other tool depends on how well you operate the mind. Every tool is as powerful as the mind that uses it. Africa is the richest continent in natural resources. Natural resources are the tools for wealth creation. Nevertheless, Africa is the poorest in terms of living standards because it has a high level of undeveloped minds.

The more developed your mind is the more productive you become. Classification of the world into first, second and third world is broadly not based on resources or infrastructure but the level of developed minds. A country will never become a first world country by improving its infrastructure but by developing the minds of the citizens through education.

Power or influence in life is not derived from positions but the capabilities of a man's mind. Less powerful minds are ruled by more powerful ones. There will be hope for Africa if our system of education is revolutionised. In July 2011, Webometrics conducted a research that assessed the performance of 12,000 universities and colleges in the world. University of Cape Town, the best university in Africa ranked 324 out of the 12,000 universities and colleges. 68 out of the world's 100 best universities are found in the United States of America. The rest of the 100 best universities are found in Europe and Asia[1]. This analogy shows that the prosperity of a nation is directly influenced by the systems developing the minds of its people.

[1] Webometrics Lab (July 2011) "Webometrics Ranking of World Universities" <www.Webometrics.info/top12000.asp >

Men are not limited by resource in their quest for achievement but their ability to use their minds. The mind has the ability to use whatever resource at its disposal to achieve its expected results.

United Arab Emirates, a country in Asia has demonstrated the unlimited power of the mind. Notwithstanding their limitation in land, they have built an island named Palm Jumeirah in the sea. The island covers an area of seven million square meters and extends six and a half kilometres (6.5kms) into the Arabian Gulf (Sea). It consists of Villas, private beaches, Canal Cove Town Home, marinas, restaurants, cafes, a variety of retail outlets and many more. Palm Jumeirah is also surrounded by Crescent Island; it forms an eleven kilometre long breakwater.

To the mind, everything can be used as a resource to achieve an aim. If one can think effectively, one will discover that there is always enough resources to achieve whatever one sets the mind to achieve.

There are two clear results from the use of everything; you either use it rightly to get the right result or you use it wrongly to get substandard result. The result an individual gets from the use of his mind should not be the standard for measuring the power of the mind. If you are not getting the right result from the use of your mind, it may be a sign that you are probably not using it the right way. To the mind everything is possible; good or bad. Perfect your skill in using your mind and you will be amazed to find that there are no limits to what you can do.

Chapter 2

The Mind As An Institution

The mind is like a governing institution and a seat of influence. The mind contains a structure that operates the human system and also governs life. The structure of the mind is broadly classified as:

- Conscious Mind
- Unconscious Mind

The Conscious Mind[2]

It is the section of the mind that initiates voluntary activities. It is more powerful compared to the Unconscious mind. The conscious mind can be likened to the coach of a football team or the board of directors of

---

[2] Harry Carpenter. (2005) Power Of Your Subconscious Mind: How it works and how to use it. San Diego: Anaphase II Publishing.

[2] Gurdip Hari (2005) The Conscious, Unconscious, & Super- Conscious Mind. Lynwood, California: Jasmin Publishing House.

an institution. This makes it the highest authority in the mind.

The conscious mind is the gate to the mind. All information received by an individual goes through the conscious mind. At the conscious section of the mind, information is sieved to differentiate the good from the bad, and how the good will be used. Information found to be useful by the mind will be customised by the conscious mind to suit it.

The conscious mind has the ability to differentiate between what is right and what is wrong at every moment based on the information at its disposal. This ability makes it a guide to the mind. As a guide, it influences the functions performed by the other parts of the mind. The conscious mind performs all its functions through thinking.

The Unconscious Mind[3]
The unconscious mind is the section of the mind that implements the decisions of the conscious mind. The

---

[3]Sigmund Freud (1856 - 1939)

unconscious mind is like an automated factory. Once the decision of the conscious mind is uploaded unto the subconscious mind, it produces the result at will.

Its ability to produce result at will gives it an involuntary character. Some involuntary activities performed by the unconscious mind are the circulation of blood in human beings and the reaction of an individual when terrified.

It is not mandatory that the unconscious mind acts on instructions created by its conscious mind alone. It can act on any information that it accesses. This flexibility makes the mind vulnerable to the adaptation and use of information that may not be beneficial to the individual.

This vulnerability of the mind, calls for a vibrant conscious mind. A vibrant conscious mind thinks through information to sift the good from the bad and the acceptable from the unacceptable. This is to determine the most beneficial course of action to be adopted by the unconscious mind.

An inactive conscious mind allows the unconscious mind access to all information encountered by the mind without evaluation. Such a mind is weak and cannot differentiate between good and bad; neither will it customise information to suit an individual's situation. People with weak minds do not think for themselves. They mostly adopt and use ideas regardless of how relevant it will be to their situation. Such a state of mind creates an individual with no focus and progression. This is one reason why skill in thinking and learning is a necessity.

The unconscious mind at birth can be likened to a computer's hard disk. It is almost empty with the exception of the instruction that controls the biological activities of the child (example: keeps the heart beating to circulate blood). These instructions it may inherit from his parents.

The programming of the unconscious mind has to be done deliberately through the conscious mind. If the programming is not done deliberately the mind will pick up behaviours which will not support a moral and ethical future. Behaviours that are accidentally adapted by the unconscious mind are mostly behaviours that are dominant in its environment. An example is when a child grows up in an environment dominated by armed robbers. There is a high tendency for the child to be an armed rubber. This is not because he wanted to but because armed robbery is the behaviour available to his unconscious mind to adopt.

The programmed unconscious mind forms the basis of the result we get in life. When events in life do not turn out the way we desire them to be, most individuals find it easier to blame it on other things, other than the mind. They rarely stop to consider the fact that they could be experiencing the desires and thoughts of their programmed minds. Wit, "as a man thinketh, so is he." One truth is that everybody can change the result he is getting in life by changing his thoughts.

It is believed that by age seven, a child would have formed most of the mental structures that will influence his life-time behaviours. This is according to Piaget's theory of Cognitive development. With this, it is logical to conclude that by age seven, a child is either programmed to stand at an advantage or a disadvantage in life. This is why the Bible admonishes Christian parents and guardians to "train up a child the way he should go so that when he grows up he will not depart from it"- Proverbs 22 v 6.

A prince is trained from childhood to think and carry himself like a king. Likewise, children should be trained to fit into the future expected of them.[4]

3Bruner (1937) Infants Cognition As The Acquisition Of Skill.

Chapter 3

The Power Of Thinking

Tools by themselves don't produce result and the mind is no exception. The more knowledge one has about the use of a tool the more prolific one becomes with the use of that tool. The most powerful tool will only achieve according to the knowledge its user has about it.

Thinking is the skill for operating the mind. It is the skill that unlocks the power of the mind. This chapter will help you understand why you need to acquire skills in thinking.

It is common to hear people say they are thinking, but surprisingly, when such people are asked what thinking is, they fumble with the answer. How then do they know they are thinking?

It is misleading to assume that everybody with a sane mind automatically thinks because thinking is not a skill that one is born with. It is a skill that is to be deliberately learnt.

What you are and what you will ever become is based on your thinking skills. No one can excel above his or her thinking skills. Thinking therefore is the creator of a man's future and the world around them. The trend of events in our world today is a product of yesterday's thinkers. The future as we all hope for is being engineered by the thoughts of men thinking today and the best of this future will be accessed by the most skillful thinkers.

The world is ruled by the thinking minority. Research conducted by Merrill Lynch and Capgemini revealed that eight and a half percentage of the world's population constitute the world's richest[5]. It is conclusive that this group of people make up the thinking minority.

---

[5] Merrill Lynch and Capgemini (2010)
http://www.wsws.org/articles/2011/jun2011/rich-j25.shtml

One cannot be part of this ruling class unless one thinks like them. No one can find his or her level in life by the dictates of a system but by the depth of their individual thoughts. There is no system that can close the gap between the rich and the poor because all humans can't think the same thoughts all the time and at the same time.

Every growing child has the dream of becoming part of the ruling class but very few make it to that level. The reason is that their dreams do not correspond with their thoughts. Most of them think their way into average life while dreaming their way to prominence.

You don't get what you dream and pray for. You get what you think about what you dream and what you pray for. Solomon, the wisest man who ever existed, is quoted in Proverbs 23:7 as saying, "...for as he thinketh in his heart, so is he." Right thoughts are the requisite for success in every endeavour.

Chapter 4

Tools For Thinking

Thinking, like other activity, require special skills. Thinking skills are the tools for thinking. Can you imagine a medical doctor who does not know the use of the stethoscope? The same way, the mind cannot be operated without knowledge of the thinking skills. They are fundamental to every thinking process.

Thinking skills can broadly be grouped as:
- Primary thinking skills
- Secondary thinking skills

Primary Thinking

Primary thinking skills are tools used to initiate thinking. Primary thinking skills thrive on questions. The questions are either open-ended or close-ended depending on the thinking process one intends to initiate.

Close-Ended Questions

These are questions that require simple, straightforward answers, usually not more than a word or a few words. Take, for example, a question like "are you going home?" The only possible answers are "yes" or "no". The answer to such a question is drawn from a decided mind or established information. This method of exploring the mind is termed convergent thinking[2].

Open-Ended Questions

These are questions that require an explanation or a conversation to answer. It is mostly used to explore new ideas or answers. Open-ended questions typically begin with the five Ws or what Rudyard Kipling calls the "Six Honest Serving Men[6]": what, why, when, how, where and who.

By extension, other phrases are used which serve the same purpose as these "six Honest Serving Men". For

---

[6] Kipling, Rudyard. "I Keep Six Honest serving Men."
http://www.kipling.org.uk/poems_serving.htm July 8, 2011

example, "tell me about….." can be used in place of "What" or "How".

Open-ended questions help to explore new information and establish the basis for new levels of thinking and research. Open ended questions spark creativity. This form of exploring the mind is termed divergent thinking[7].

Secondary Thinking Skills

Secondary thinking skills evolve from the use of the primary thinking skills to achieve a purpose. There could be several secondary thinking skills but the ones known to the writer have been explained below:

- Critical Thinking
- Inductive Thinking
- Deductive thinking
- Analytical Thinking
- Concept
- Segment
- Imagination
- Picture Thinking
- Practical Interpretation

---

[7] Hudson (1966) Cognitive Styles.

- Counter-examples

Critical Thinking

Critical thinking is used to assess ideas. The assessment is done to confirm the validity or pointlessness of an idea. It is used when assessing the validity of a thing against a set objectives or standards. Critical thinking is not necessarily negative. It sometimes leads to positive conclusion about an idea. Critical thinking is made possible by close-ended questions (convergent thinking).

Example of a critical thought is the assessment of the performance of a government with reference to its campaign promises. Upon assessing the government, shortcomings are either discovered or its performance applauded. Critical thinking set the stage for creativity.

Inductive Thinking

Inductive thinking is a skill for gathering information about an idea. It involves asking questions as to where and how information can be obtained about an idea. Such information can be sourced from examples that have relevance to the idea in question. Books and observing activities being undertaken is also a good source for gathering information.

Deductive Thinking

Deductive thinking is a skill used to draw conclusions from gathered information. The quality of one's conclusions depends on the quality of information the individual has gathered through inductive thinking. Here is an example:

Kojo is a qualified accountant.

His wife Deborah is a medical doctor.

They live in a first class neighbourhood.

Their three children school in an expensive university.

A conclusion that can be made from the information above is that: this family is rich.

Analytical Thinking

It is a thinking mechanism used to investigate the composition of an idea. Analytical thinking has two main uses: a segregative and a comparative use.

Segregative Analysis

It is a technique for separating an idea into the parts that make up that idea. Example, segregative analysis can be used to identify the parts that make up the word bird as follows: the head, neck, tail, wings, legs, feet, feathers, beck, eyes and others.

Comparative Analysis

Comparative analysis is a technique used to draw a relationship between the parts that constitute an idea. This is done by finding the reasons why an idea or word has a particular group of parts as it constitutes.

In the case of the word bird; comparative analysis is used to find the reason why a bird should have a head, wings, tail, legs, feet, feathers, beck but not teeth, hands and nails as its constitute parts. Information got through comparative analysis helps one to understand the function of an idea or a word.

Concept

A concept describes the function of a word or an idea. Concepts are formed to get better understanding of words or ideas. To form a concept about a word, one must know what its constituted components are, and how the various components function.

Let us use the word bird to illustrate the understanding of a concept. Some of the components of the word bird are wings, feathers, legs, tail, feet and neck. By knowing the functions of a bird's wings (for flying) and legs (for landing), one can deduce a concept that, a bird is a living thing that flies.

The more components we uncover about a word or an idea, coupled with their functions, the better we understand that word.

Segment

Components of words or ideas have subcomponents. These subcomponents can be called segment. Segments give more information about the component of a word. The component, leg, of the word bird, for example, has scales, flesh, joint, etc as its segment.

Component and segments of words or ideas are the windows to learning. The further one analyses an object of study into its components and segments, the better that individual can understand it.

Imagination

We relate to the world through our senses. Data or information is transferred from the world to us through our senses. They are the sense of touch, sight, smell, hear and taste. The imagination coalesces the information from our senses into images for the mind to understand. These images form our perception of the world. It is with our perceptions that we interpret the world.

Imagination is a research tool of the mind. The limit to which one can acquire knowledge is equal to the limit to which his imagination can create images to represent his perceptions. One's knowledge ends where his imagination ends. "Imagination is better than knowledge"- Thomas Edison.

The power of the imagination is limited by natural principles. Products of the imagination become an illusion if they violate natural laws.

Picture Thinking

We learn and think with words. Words are abstract elements. The abstract nature of words makes learning and thinking a challenge for the mind. This is so because the mind recognises things the ear hears but gives attention to things the eye sees. To get the attention of the mind to learn new things, one has to present it in a picture form. Picture thinking can either be used as a learning tool or a teaching tool.

Let us consider picture thinking as a tool for learning. Every word creates a picture. The picture of a word is deduced when we analyse a word into its components and segments. This is done with the intent on finding out how the parts of the word function as a unit. The meaning of the word bird is deduced when one tries to employ its component such as wings, tail, legs, feet, neck and head to perform their independent functions. For example, picturing a bird jump into the sky and flap its wings will give you an idea that a bird is a living thing that fly. Picture thinking is a technique that brings learning from an abstract world into reality.

Let us consider picture thinking as a tool for teaching. The Bible has countless scenarios of God using pictures to attract, teach and bring understanding to His servants. Abraham's encounter with God captured in Genesis 15:5 is an example of such an instance. "And he brought him forth abroad, and said, Look now toward heaven, and tell the stars, if thou be able to number them: and he said unto him, So shall thy seed be."

It was easy for Abraham to understand the extent to which God wanted to bless him through the illustration, using stars.

What we see has an effect on what we choose to think about and what we think about has an effect on what we see. Hearing is of little influence in learning or thinking if one cannot create images to represent what one hears. The more vivid pictures we can reveal about what we hear the better the mind brings us understanding.

Practical Interpretation

Practical interpretation is a technique that seeks to give a meaning to a word or an idea in a way that mirrors the experience we expect from that word. By extension, practical interpretation seeks to prescribe the meaning of words to fit its real life application. Practical interpretation of a word goes beyond its dictionary explanation.

Detail questioning is a technique required to bring out the practical or experiential meaning of a word. Words like how, why and what, are mostly employed in the technique of detail questioning. For example, if the question "what does it mean to organise?" is asked. One may answer: to organise means to make an arrangement so that an activity can happen effectively. Follow-up question: how can one make an arrangement that will make an activity happen effectively? This follow up question is necessary because the answer given does not prescribe an activity that fit the meaning of the word in real life term.

In real life terms "to organise" means to group substances with similar characteristics for a purpose. This meaning mirrors the experience we expect from the word "organise" in real life.

Practical interpretation is the bridge between an idea and its realisation. Lack of practical understanding to words makes it difficult for people to execute ideas.

Counter-examples

Counter exampling involves the use of several examples to illustrate the different shades of meanings that a word can possess. The reason for this action is to determine an exclusive meaning for that word.

Let us illustrate the method of counter-examples with what the meaning of the word banana is.

Mamaa ask a question: what is banana?

Kojo answers: banana is a fruit.

Mamaa comes up with a counter-example: an orange is also a fruit, does that mean an orange is a kind of banana?

Sometimes we think we know, when in reality, we do not know. Counter-exampling is one tool that will help us expose our ignorance. Counter-examples help us to refine our understandings of issues. It does not always lead you to the exclusive meaning of a word. Nevertheless, one will still benefit as it will bring a deeper understanding of the word.

Chapter 5

The Art Of Thinking

Thinking is defined as an activity of the mind that controls thought consciously or unconsciously and manipulates information to produce result[8]. The focus of this study is on conscious thoughts and its ability to solve problems. The success of thinking depends on the effective use of the thinking tools.

The activities that make up a thinking process for solving a problem are:
- Control of Thought
- Concept Definition
- Processes for Thinking

The above thinking activities can be used to solve every human problem.

[8] Eysenck and Keane (1995)

Control of Thoughts

Every word contains an idea that can spark a thinking process. To avoid every word sparking a new thinking process in the mind, one has to clearly define what one wants to think about and consciously create a thinking pattern that will support one's defined thought. In other words, one cannot put a ceiling on the nature and number of thoughts generated in his mind through words but can effectively control them.

The control of thoughts begins with the interpretation of words with reference to a specific focus. If the ideas in the word are contrary to your preferred thoughts delete it and choose another word that supports what you are thinking about. Controlling thought is one way of sustaining a thinking process.

The thoughts of how important education is, for instance, can be sustained when every word that deliberately or otherwise makes its way into the mind is interpreted in connection to how important education is.

Concepts Definition

Concept definition is a process of defining the result one expects from a thinking process. Studies on thinking reveal that concept definition in respect to thinking involves:

- Definition of an Idea and
- Perception Development

Definition of an Idea

An idea is defined by deciding on what the components and characteristics of a product should be. A decision to build an airplane that will carry 100 passengers instead of 150 is an example of how an idea is defined.

New ideas are formed when knowledge acquired through learning is put to different use. The idea of an airplane for instance is the diversification of the knowledge acquired through the study of how birds fly. A well defined idea takes ambiguity out of a thinking process and sets the stage for effective thinking.

Perception Development

Perception is what one thinks is real with reference to a situation or an idea. It is either negative or positive. Life as an idea, sparks many perceptions. Some of the perceptions are as follows:

- Life is not fair,
- Certain great positions in life belongs to a particular group of people,
- Life is a race and only the swift can win.

One's perception about an idea determines one's attitude towards it. An individual holding a perception that, certain positions in life belong to particular group of people; will be reluctant to aspire to those positions.

Perceptions form the basis of one's thought and determines what one thinks is possible or not. What we perceive to be impossible becomes the limitation on our thinking process and our future. Limitations are therefore not based upon reality but negative perceptions.

One must therefore be careful to develop a personal philosophy that sees everything to be possible in life so as to live above limitation.

Processes for Thinking

The end result of thinking is to solve a problem. The single or combined use of primary and secondary thinking skills forms the various processes for thinking. The processes for thinking are the methods employed in thinking to solve problems. It is the last activity that completes a thinking process. It follows after one has decided on the problem one wants to solve at the end of a thinking process.

The processes of thinking can be likened to the production of tomatoes. The tomatoes to be produced are the expected outcome from the thinking process while the activities (weeding, irrigation, etc.) that produce the tomato farm and eventually the fruit are the thinking processes to be employed.

The processes for thinking can be broadly divided into two. These two are:
- Basic methods for thinking
- Complex method for thinking

More about these two are contained in the next two chapters.

Chapter 6

Basic Methods Of Thinking

Basic methods of thinking are the thinking processes that are used to solve the common problems we encounter daily. The problems of interpretation, creativity, progression, constructiveness and correlation are assumed by the writer to be the five common problems that we come across daily. These five problems can be solved through the use of the following basic methods of thinking:

- Interpretative Thinking
- Progressive Thinking
- Constructive Thinking
- Creative Thinking
- Correlative Thinking

There are no strict sequences for applying thinking skills to these basic methods of thinking.

Interpretative Thinking

Interpretative thinking is a process used to discover the meaning of an idea. Interpretation can take many forms. It could be contextual, manipulative and extrapolative. Two among the many forms of interpretative thinking are explained below – contextual and extrapolative interpretation.

Contextual Interpretation
Contextual interpretation is applied to find the true meaning of an idea based on how it is used in a particular situation. The true meaning of an idea is determined by the information the idea wants to communicate to its listeners in a particular situation. Note that there could be several meaning to an idea but the true meaning of that idea is based on the reason why that idea is being communicated.

Proverbs 24:30 "I went by the field of the slothful, and by the vineyard of the man void of understanding;"
Proverbs 24:31 "And, lo, it was all grown over with thorns, and nettles had covered the face thereof, and the stone wall thereof was broken down".

The quotation above can be used to illustrate contextual interpretation. The true meaning of the quotation above as intended by the writer is to: advise its readers that anyone who is slothful and lacks understanding cannot take care of a vineyard or farm.

Extrapolative Interpretation
Extrapolative interpretation is a process used to find out what the outcome will be if a particular idea is pictured in a different situation. An example is to think of how it will be like if Osama Bin-laden becomes the head of the United Nations. Extrapolative interpretation is achieved by asking question using phrases like "what if...." and "what will happen...."

Progressive Thinking
Progressive thinking is a thought designed to make an individual adapt a life style that will make him always think of ways to bring improvements in any situation. Progressive thinking does not give in to the idea that once a problem has been solved, it is forgotten or to the notion that "if it isn't broken don't fix it". A progressive thinker's attitude is that "there is always room for improvement". In progressive thinking, creative thinking is always used to examine and initiate changes that will make a situation better.

Constructive Thinking

This is a process designed to make individuals continuously add and modify the understanding they have about a subject. In constructive thinking, no established understanding about a subject is accepted as final. In constructive thinking, new information are continually collected and examined to better one's understanding about a subject. Inductive, analytical and deductive thinking are used in constructive thinking.

Creative Thinking

Creative thinking is an ability to combine ideas to meet a need. It is applied when one wants to improve on already existing idea or generate original ideas. The creation of the airplane by the Wright brothers and the telephone by Graham Bell are examples of creative thinking. All creative thoughts require the use of open-ended questions.

"How can we reduce the production costs in this company without reducing our production levels?" is an example of a question that calls for creativity. The answer to such a question calls for new forms of information to answer it.

Creative thinking is carried out through several thoughts. We can arrive at each creative idea by using one or more of the thoughts below:

Evolutional Thought

This method of creative thinking seeks to improve on old ideas. New ideas stem from other ideas, new solutions from previous ones with the new ideas being an improvement over the old ones. Many sophisticated things enjoyed today developed gradually from simple ideas.

The history of cars is an example of evolutional thoughts. Each new model is built on the improvement on old models. This brings improvement in economy, comfort and elegance. The improvements that determines the difference between 2011 s-class Mercedes Benz and a 1970 s-class Mercedes Benz is an example of evolutional thoughts.

Synthesised Thought

This is a method of creative thinking where two or more existing ideas are combined to form a third idea. Combining the idea of a magazine and an audiotape births the idea of a magazine that can be listened to. This will be beneficial to the blind and other individuals.

Revolutionary Thought

This is a method of creative thinking that seeks to produce new ideas. Such ideas have no resemblance with other ideas. The idea to use gas as an alternative energy to petrol in cars is an example of creativity through revolution.

Reapplicative Thought

Reapplicative thought is a form of creative thinking that looks out for different ways to use an idea. The aim of reapplicative thought is to see beyond the original application for an idea, in order to use it for other purposes. An example is the use of cooking oil for a job that requires grease.

Oriental Thought

This is a creative thought that shifts attention from a particular way of solving a problem in other ways. The economy of China is an example of creativity through oriental thoughts. The Chinese economy is flourishing under a democratic government that is different from the Western type of democracy.

Correlative Thinking

This is a process of thinking that seeks to find a relationship between two or more statements connected to a particular subject. The relationship between the statements could be negative or positive.

Here is an example to illustrate correlative thinking:
Jesus Christ is a descendant of David.
Jesus Christ was born by a virgin by name Mary.
Joseph the husband of Mary is a descendant of David, Mary is not.

The puzzle between the above three statements is how Jesus Christ could be the descendant of David when Joseph the one who is the descendant of David played no biological role in the birth of Jesus Christ. To solve such puzzle new information that has links to these statements need to be sort.

After researching for more information to solve the puzzle, the writer came across this: Psalm 127:3 "children are a gift from the Lord" (Good News Bible).

Conclusion: if children are gifts from God then children are not a product of sex. If children are gifts then it does not matter how one gets them – The mode of delivering a gift does not change the one who the gift is addressed to. Based on this new information, one can conclude that Jesus is the son of Joseph and a descendant of David.

Correlative thinking will mostly result in a negative conclusion if the information gathered about the statement is sketchy. Answers to correlative thoughts that involves matters of the Bible, should best be sorted through the guidance of the Holy Spirit.

Chapter 7

Complex Method Of Thinking

The complex method of thinking is a thinking process of solving difficult problems. Problems such as "how to build a ship, airplane and solve the economic challenges of a nation" will require thinking processes that are more complex than the Basic methods of thinking.

The basic methods of thinking and the tools of thinking are the skills needed to operate the complex method of thinking. There is no preferred sequence of using the tools for thinking and the basic methods of thinking in the complex method of thinking process. We will use Yankson's Model of complex thinking to illustrate complex method of thinking.

<u>Yankson's Model Of Complex Thinking</u>

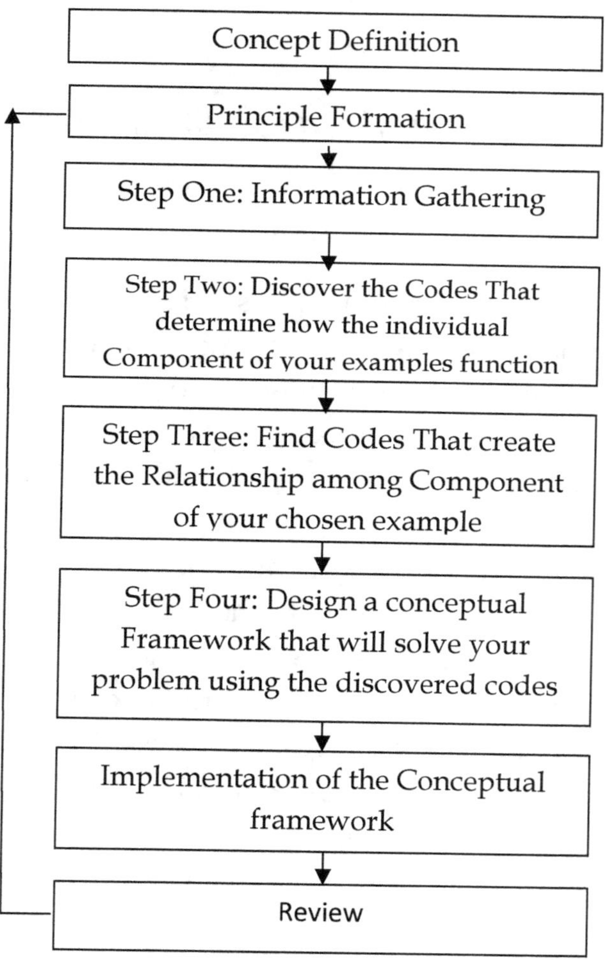

This model was designed by Kojo Kronzuwa Yankson. The steps that make up the complex method of thinking are explained below.

Concept Definition

This entails defining the problem one wants to solve or what one intend to achieve after the complex thinking process. The process for defining a concept was explained in chapter five. Reference can be made to it if necessary. We will use how to build an airplane as our case study to illustrate how to solve a complex problem using Yankson's Model of complex thinking.

Principle Formation[9]

Principle formation is an activity to discover the codes that will determine how to solve our problem (build an airplane). A code is the reason that makes an activity feasible. To develop a code that will solve one's problem, codes in examples that are similar to the problem one want to solve are discovered and modify to suit ones

---

[9] Craig Rusbult, Ph.D. An Overview of Thinking Skills. Retrieved from: http://asa3.org/asa/education/think/skills.htm May, 2004

situation. There are four steps that make up the principle formation process.

Step One - Information Gathering

Observation, interviewing people and books are some of the sources to gather information about examples that have similar solutions to the problem we want to solve. The imagination is used to gather information by creating pictures, in situations where physical images of the object of study do not exist.

Let us use "how birds fly" as the example to illustrate how to gather information in order to solve a problem (build an airplane). To gather information about how birds fly, one will first have to list the components and segments of the bird that enable it to fly. Examples of such parts are: the wings, the feet, the tail, the neck, the head and the feathers.

Detailed information about the characteristics and functions of these parts are then gathered. It is based on information about the characteristics and functions of components and segments of a subject that codes governing the subject can be discovered.

Step Two : Discover The Codes That Determine How The Individual Component Of Your Examples Function

After information has been gathered, right questions need to be asked to be able to discover the needed codes. One of such questions is "why a bird flaps its wings in order to fly?". Answer to such a question can be arrived at by carefully examining the information gathered about a bird and the influence its environment has on it.

It can be deduced from the information about a bird that, a bird flaps its wings so it can push air downwards, producing an opposite force that will lift the bird into the air. Pushing air downwards, to produce an opposite force that will lift the bird into the air is the reason or code governing the flapping of the wings by the bird.

Another question that can be asked is "why big birds run against the wind before it jumps with its legs and fly?". In this situation, the reason why the bird runs against the wind before it jumps and fly, is for it to generate enough energy that will neutralise the force of the wind acting against it. The bird can then fly after it has neutralised the force of the wind acting against it. The code or the reason why a bird should run against the wind before it flies is to be able to generate enough speed that will neutralize the force of the wind.

Step Three: Find Codes That Create The Relationship Among Components Of Your Chosen Example

This step is designed to determine the codes that create a relationship between two or more independent component. Let us illustrate this by finding the code that creates the relationship between the activities of the wings and the activities of the legs of the bird.

Some independent activities undertaken by the wings and the legs are the flapping of the wings and the jumping into the air respectively. To determine the codes that create a relationship between - the flapping of the wings and the jumping into the air – the right questions need to be asked. One of such questions is "why the bird has to jump into the air and flap its wings before its fly?". After careful examination of the characteristics of these two activities using analytical thinking, it can be concluded that the bird jumps into the air to create space between its body and the ground, which allows the bird to flap its wings in order to takeoff.

The codes or reasons discovered in activities two and three is what will be used to create the activities or laws that will be used to create and operate a conceptual framework to solve the problem we intend to solve. Conceptual Framework is a plan that identifies the parts and the laws that will regulate these parts to solve a problem.[10]

Step Four: Design A Conceptual Framework That Will Solve Your Problem Using The Discovered Codes From Your Examples

In developing a conceptual framework, the information gathered is examined with the intention of finding the parts and the activities that need to work together to solve our problem. To create our airplane, the codes that were discovered in the study of the bird will be used to create parts and activities that will form its conceptual frame work. Let us illustrate how the codes discovered

---

[10] Prof. Robert N. Anthony (1965) Planning And Control: A framework for analysis. Boston.

above can be used to develop parts and activities to operate the conceptual framework of an airplane.

The code behind the flapping of the wings by the bird is to generate enough force for the bird to fly. This code if applied to the creation of an airplane, will lead to the creation of the engines and the wings of the airplane. The engines on the wings of the airplane are to serve the purpose of generating enough force for the airplane to take off.

The code behind the running of the bird against the wind before it flies is meant to generate energy that will neutralise the force of the wind so that it can fly. This code, if applied to the creation of an airplane, will lead to the creation of the tyre of the airplane. -The tyre is used to run against the wind; neutralising the force acting against the airplane so it can take off.

Implementation of the Conceptual Framework[3]
This is the process for projecting a result from the conceptual framework that has been developed based on its codes.

This happens by using the codes of the conceptual framework to project an activity that will equal the solution one wants to achieve through the imagination. The projection of an outcome should be done in phases before the whole is applied.

Review of Result

At the review stage, critical thinking is used to evaluate the projected result against the defined expected result. This mental activity involves the assessment of the extent to which the expected solution has been achieved.

Based on the assessment, possible causes of errors in the result of the thinking process will be detected so that corrective measures are instituted through the principled formative processes. The process is repeated until a desired result is achieved.

The activities that make up the complex method of thinking can be applied to solve any problem: creating a new dance, solving a marriage problem, creating a company, starting a church, governing a country, manufacturing something and many others that you can think off. If the result achieved from the thinking process is not what one expects, adjustment should be made to the – Problem definition, principle formation, implementation of the conceptual framework, and review activities till the expected result is achieved.

Note: there are situations where examples that can be used as a base to solve a problem will not exist. In such situations, one has to use the imagination through practical interpretation and picture thinking to form an image of the desired result. This will help you to gather information to work on the principle formative processes.

Chapter 8

The Essence Of Learning

Thinking thrives on knowledge. The knowledge of an individual in a particular discipline of study makes him an authority over someone. The more knowledgeable you are the more creative and powerful you are with your thought. Knowledge is acquired by learning.

Learning reorients the mind to shift from producing one kind of result to another. It is the bridge between the wise and the foolish, the strong and the weak, the rich and the poor, the righteous and the unrighteous, the superior and the inferior. It is the practical activity that stands between one state of being and another. No man can undergo any change without learning. You can change only to the extent that you have learnt.

The essence of learning is to get educated. Learning in this context encompasses both formal, informal and intuitive[7]. People confuse schooling or receiving education with when one becomes educated. Schooling is one of the many platforms meant to educate people. A man can go through schooling and not get educated. At what point is an individual educated? It is a state where an individual acquires the ability to identify and prescribe a solution to a problem in an area of study. A man ceases to be educated when new problems emerge which he has no solution to. In such a situation, the man should go back to learn till he can solve that problem. This explains the saying: "education has no end".

The British colonised the Gold Coast, now Ghana. Years after colonisation, many in Ghana began to campaign to re-gain independence. The struggle for independence was ineffective until some Ghanaians became educated.

These educated Ghanaians made the struggle for independence more progressive. J.E Casely Hayford, Dr. J.B Danquah and Dr. Kwame Nkrumah were among the educated Ghanaians who joined the struggle for independence. Dr. Nkrumah formed the Convention

People's Party and later went ahead to become the first Prime Minister of Ghana after his party won the general election.

The battle for independence in Ghana and Africa as a whole was not won by chance. It was won when men like Dr. Nkrumah, Mr. Mugabe, Mr. Nelson Mandela and others became educated to compete with their colonial masters. This analogy concerning how Ghana and the other African countries attained independence is to place emphasis on the fact that, you will only fix a problem when you are educated about it. The scripture below buttresses this fact. Galatians 4:1-2 "Now I say, that the heir, as long as he is a child, differeth nothing from a servant, though he be lord of all; But is under tutors and governors until the time appointed of the father".

We will become educated by either going through the formal schooling system or by self-tuition. In both ways, ones result is the only prove that one is educated. Abraham Lincoln, Malcolm X and Albert Einstein are great individuals whose rise to prominence was driven largely by self-tuition. It is said that Malcolm X took a job that paid less in order that he could get more time to study. Malcolm X became the second most influential public speaker in America.

How much benefit an individual gets from education depends on the type of mind that is educating that individual. The greater the mind an individual interacts with the better developed the individual's mind becomes. This brightens the prospect of that individual's future.

God has a mind that no human mind can imagine. Recognising the mind of God as supreme and making it your source of education is fundamental in building an unusual mind.

We interact with the mind of individuals through their thoughts. The Bible is the thoughts of God in print. The more we study the Bible the more we interact with the thoughts of God and the more developed our minds become. King Solomon, the wisest man to live on earth, explains this wisdom in Proverbs 28:5 "Evil men understand not judgment: but they that seek the LORD understand all things".

Great opportunities come to educated men. We lack great opportunities because we are not educated. Education for that matter learning, is the fundamental tool for birthing new ideas. Every new idea creates a new opportunity.

Chapter 9

The Art Of Learning

Reading is not equal to learning. Learning goes beyond reading. It is a procedure for training the mind to perform a task. How every task is preformed is rooted in a mindset. A mindset is an organised thought of producing a specific result. By extension, learning is a procedure for adapting the mindset of performing a specific task. The ability to duplicate what one has learnt is a proof that one has completed the learning process.

There are three forms of learning: the rationalist approach[11], empiricist approach[12] and intuitive approach[13]. The rationalist approach uses reason to deduce the understanding of a subject. The empiricist approach uses experiment   to   deduce   the   understanding

---

[11] Henri Bergson (1859-1941)

[12] Rene Descartes (1596-1650). John Locke (1632- 1702), George Berkeley (1685-1753).

[13] Henri Bergson (1859-1941)

of a subject. The intuitive approach relies on instincts to acquire the understanding of a subject. These three approaches complement each other at some point. The focus of our study is the rationalist approach to learning. Its application will be explained using Yankson's Subject Decoding Model (YSD Model).

<u>Yankson's Subject Decoding Model</u>

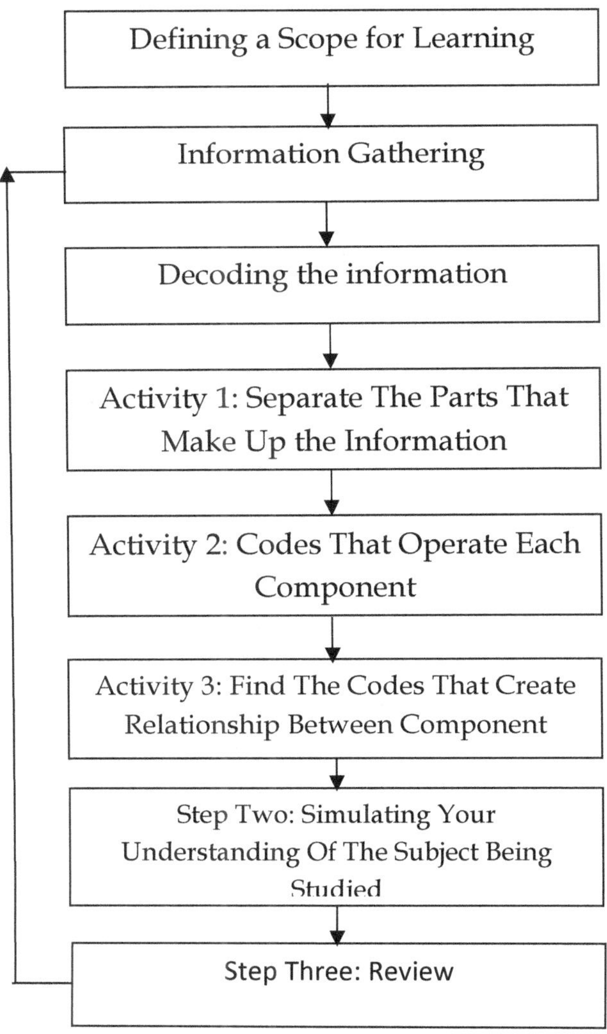

Details of the model have been explained below.

Defining a Scope for Learning

Defining a scope for learning involves determining the extent of knowledge one wants to acquire about a subject. Appropriate definition of a scope determines the kind of information and resources to gather for that learning activity.

Let us illustrate how to define a scope for learning using bird as an example. There are many things that can be studied about the subject bird. Example: how a bird fly, the reproductive system of a bird and how a bird sleeps. To make learning more precise and also take away ambiguity, a specific area to study should be chosen at a time.

Information Gathering

The components and the segments of a subject of study form the basis of gathering information. Observation, interviewing people and books are some of the sources to gather information. The imagination is used to gather information by creating pictures, in situations where physical images of the object of study do not exist.

Let us choose the subject: "how birds fly" to illustrate how to gather information. To gather information, about how birds fly, one will first have to list the components and segments of the bird that enable it to fly. Examples of such parts are: the wings, the feet, the tail, the neck, the head and the feathers.

Detailed information about the characteristics and functions of these parts need to be gathered, for additional work to be done to achieve understanding of the subject being studied (how birds fly). It is based on information about the components and segments of a subject that codes governing the subject can be discovered.

Decoding the Information

A code is the reason for performing an activity. By extension, a code is a law that regulates a single or batch of activities. Questions that begin with "why" is usually what is needed to uncover a code.

Discovery of codes leads to the understanding of a subject. Example, when the law of gravity was discovered people came to understand why object tossed into the air fall back unto the earth. The process of decoding information may involve three steps.

Step One

This step may involve three activities. They are as follows:

1. Use analytical thinking to separate the parts that make up the subjects being studied into its components and segments.
2. Use comparative analysis, inductive and deductive thinking to find the codes that determine how the activities of the individual components and segments should work.
3. Use analytical and deductive thinking to find the codes that operate the relationship that exist between independent activities.

Let us use the subject, how birds fly to illustrate the three activities that make up step one of decoding information.

Step One, Activity One

In this activity, analytical thinking is used to examine the bird into the components and segments that make up a bird. Some of these components are: wings, legs, feet, tail and feathers. We then separate the parts that play a role in how a bird flies from the other parts. The parts that play a role in how birds fly are grouped for additional work to be done on it.

Step One, Activity Two
In this activity, comparative analysis is used to find out the codes that operate the individual components of the bird that enable it to fly. The right questions need to be asked to find these codes. One of such questions is why a bird flaps its wings in order to fly? After careful examination of the characteristics of the wings of a bird, a conclusion that can be made about why a bird flaps its wings before it flies is this: to push air downwards, producing an opposite force that will lift the bird into the air.

Another question that can be asked is Why the bird jumps before its fly? After careful examination of the characteristics of the legs of a bird in relation to why the bird jumps before it flies is that: the bird must jump before it flies in order to generate a force that will lift it from the ground into the air.

Step One, Activity Three
In this activity, analytical and deductive thinking is used to find out the codes that create the relationship between these two independent activities - the flapping of the

wings and the jumping with the legs by the bird when it wants to fly. The code is this: the bird must jump so that it can create enough space between the ground and its body allowing the wings to flap and generate energy to take off.

Total knowledge about all the codes that govern the parts of a subject brings total understanding of that subject.

Step Two: Simulating Your Understanding Of The Subject Being Studied

At this step, the imagination is used to project a meaning from the subject being studied based on the codes discovered from step one. This is achieved by putting together the parts of the subjects based on your discovered codes with the intention of producing an example (clone) that will express the meaning of the subject being studied. Example, for one to know that he has understood how birds fly, one should be able to use the understanding (codes) gained from the study of the subject "how birds fly" to create an object that will fly like the bird: airplane. The result you get will be the proof that you have understood the subject you are studying. You can also check if you have understood what you have learnt by explaining it using different examples.

Step Three: Review

It is possible that the codes discovered in step two above may not be the actual codes that determine the meaning of the subject being studied. At this stage, critical and comparative analysis is used to figure out if the example projected in step two has the same meaning as the one embedded in the subject being studied. Uniformity between the two is the evidence that the subject being studied has been understood. If there are differences between the two, the information gathering and decoding process is repeated till the subject being studied is understood.

Chapter 10

Maximising The Power Of The Mind

Every tool is designed to perform best under certain conditions. The mind is no exception. Some conditions which facilitates the performance of the mind are elaborated below.

Training
Training is an activity aimed at equipping an individual with a skill to perform a task. Training can be formal or informal. The academic system is the formal tool for training.

The ultimate aim of every academic system is to get individuals educated in a specific profession. This aim is achieved through constant training over an average period of twenty years in the academic system. The academic system consists of education from the nursery level to the university or the technical level. Even after completing the academic system, training through workshops are undertaken to guarantee one's performance on the field. This is because skills fade or become obsolete without improvement.

Improvement through training guarantees one's progress in every area of life. The progress associated with training can be likened to riding a bicycle. You progress more when you ride more but come to a halt when you stop riding. Training is not an event but a life time activity. Let us seek more education about the mind so that we will be progressive with its use.

Practise

Practise is a deliberate act to repeat an activity with the intension of perfecting your skill in that activity. Practise brings progress and eventual perfection in performance. One becomes progressive with his skills when he varies its use. We must grow our skills by gradually moving from using it to solve simple problems to more complex problems. Our improved skills make us more productive.

The progression that practise brings is reflected in every discipline of life. Poor people or nations practise and grow in their ability to beg for help while the rich practise and grow in their ability to meet the needs of the poor and the world. This is one reason why the gap between the rich and the poor is most of the time widening.

We can change our fortunes by changing our practises. The fortunes of China have changed in recent times from a third world country to a major contender for the position of the world super power due to their change in practise.

All the explanations and illustrations given are to make us understand that we need to practise the skill of using the mind in order to grow and perfect it. As we grow and perfect the use of our mind it will automatically reflect in all areas of our lives.

Information
The operations of the mind are fueled by information. Information feed the mind, controls its operations and determines the kind of result it produces. "Proverbs 13:20

"He that walketh with wise men shall be wise: but a companion of fools shall be destroyed."

No standard mind is better than the other except for the information it is exposed to. Without information, the mind is reduced to a worthless tool. Hosea 4:6 "My people are destroyed for lack of knowledge..." The information supplied to the mind, engineers its transformation from one level of value to another.

One has to be particular about the information one encounters, because it may be beneficial to the progress of that individual. Information from superior minds will guarantee you superior results. The Bible contains the most superior information in the entire world. It is God's mind in print. Your understanding of the Bible will guarantee you an enviable future. Richard Nixon, the 37th president of the United States of America, once said: (studying the Bible is better than a college degree).

Spirituality
Spirituality is a state of having a relationship with spiritual entities or the spiritual world. It does not mean

being superstitious. The spiritual world is supreme to the physical world.

Our relationship with the spiritual world is to enhance our life as natural men. Supremacy of a sort is enjoyed by men who connect to the spiritual world.

History has proven that the most celebrated leaders in the world have had the root of their impact in spirituality. The outstanding wisdom through which they mesmerised the world came through spiritual inspiration.

Jesus Christ, the saviour of the world and head of the Church is the most prominent example of the men that impacted the world through spirituality. Others are: Mohammed, the founder of Islam and Siddhartha Gautama, the founder of Buddhism. The list will not be completed without mentioning Isaac Newton and some scientists and philosophers who doubled either as priests or theologians – Otto Brunfels a botanist and a theologian, Nicolaus Copernicus, an astronomer, physician, a priest etc.

The level of impact exerted by individuals with spiritual connection depends on the spirits they are relating to and the depth of relationship they have with those spirits. Among the many spirits is the Lord, the father of Jesus Christ. He is the custodian of all wisdom and understanding. He gives wisdom and understanding to all that connect to Him and follow Him in obedience.

Other Books By The Author:

- The Journey From Wakanda To Wakanda

- Who Controls The Earth - God or The Devil?